Hungry Sharks

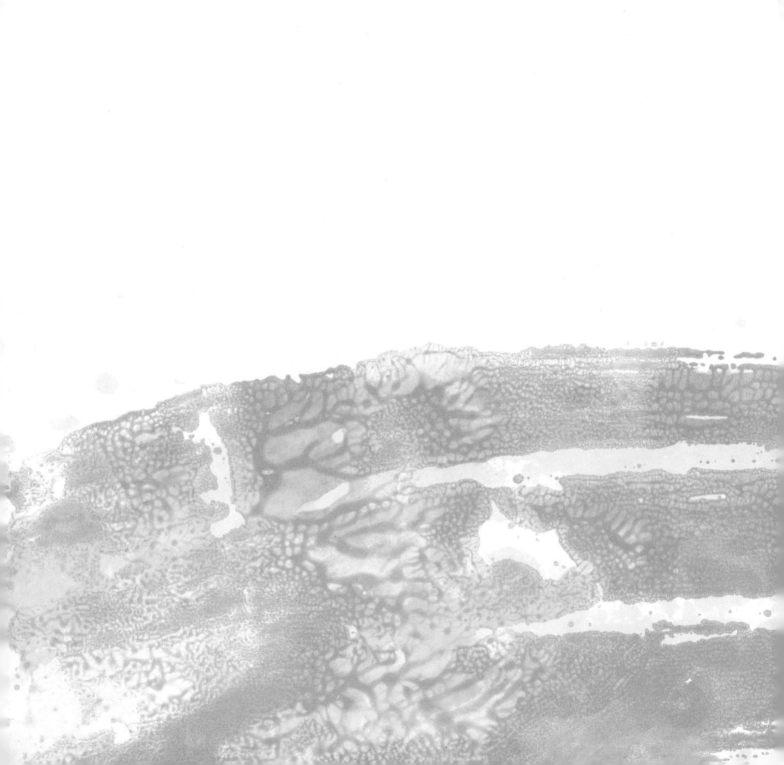

Hungry Sharks

by John F. Waters
illustrated by Ann Dalton

Thomas Y. Crowell Company

New York

LET'S-READ-AND-FIND-OUT SCIENCE BOOKS

Editors: *DR. ROMA GANS*, Professor Emeritus of Childhood Education, Teachers College, Columbia University
DR. FRANKLYN M. BRANLEY, Astronomer Emeritus and former Chairman of The American Museum—Hayden Planetarium

LIVING THINGS: PLANTS

Corn Is Maize: The Gift of the Indians
Down Come the Leaves
How a Seed Grows
Mushrooms and Molds
Plants in Winter
Redwoods Are the Tallest Trees in the World
Roots Are Food Finders
Seeds by Wind and Water
The Sunlit Sea
A Tree Is a Plant
Water Plants
Where Does Your Garden Grow?

LIVING THINGS: ANIMALS, BIRDS, FISH, INSECTS, ETC.

Animals in Winter
Bats in the Dark
Bees and Beelines
Big Tracks, Little Tracks
Birds at Night
Birds Eat and Eat and Eat
Bird Talk
The Blue Whale
Camels: Ships of the Desert
Cockroaches: Here, There, and Everywhere

Corals
Ducks Don't Get Wet
The Eels' Strange Journey
The Emperor Penguins
Fireflies in the Night
Giraffes at Home
Green Grass and White Milk
Green Turtle Mysteries
Hummingbirds in the Garden
Hungry Sharks
It's Nesting Time
Ladybug, Ladybug, Fly Away Home
Little Dinosaurs and Early Birds
The Long-Lost Coelacanth and Other Living Fossils
The March of the Lemmings
My Daddy Longlegs
My Visit to the Dinosaurs
Opossum
Sandpipers
Shells Are Skeletons
Shrimps
Spider Silk
Spring Peepers
Starfish
Twist, Wiggle, and Squirm: A Book About Earthworms
Watch Honeybees with Me
What I Like About Toads
Why Frogs Are Wet

Wild and Woolly Mammoths

THE HUMAN BODY

A Baby Starts to Grow
Before You Were a Baby
A Drop of Blood
Fat and Skinny
Find Out by Touching
Follow Your Nose
Hear Your Heart
How Many Teeth?
How You Talk
In the Night
Look at Your Eyes*
My Five Senses
My Hands
The Skeleton Inside You
Sleep Is for Everyone
Straight Hair, Curly Hair*
Use Your Brain
What Happens to a Hamburger
Your Skin and Mine*

And other books on AIR, WATER, AND WEATHER; THE EARTH AND ITS COMPOSITION; ASTRONOMY AND SPACE; and MATTER AND ENERGY
*Available in Spanish

Library of Congress Cataloging in Publication Data. Waters, John Frederick, 1930-   Hungry sharks. (Let's-read-and-find-out science book). SUMMARY: A brief introduction to the physical characteristics and habits of the shark.   1. Sharks—Juv. lit.   [1. Sharks]   I. Dalton, Ann, illus.   II. Title.   QL638.9.W38   597'.31   72-7563   ISBN 0-690-01121-0 (CQR)

6   7   8   9   10

Hungry Sharks

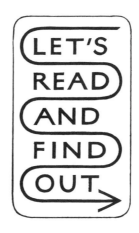

Sharks are fish. They are big eaters. They eat other fish.

They eat penguins and seals. Sharks even eat other sharks.

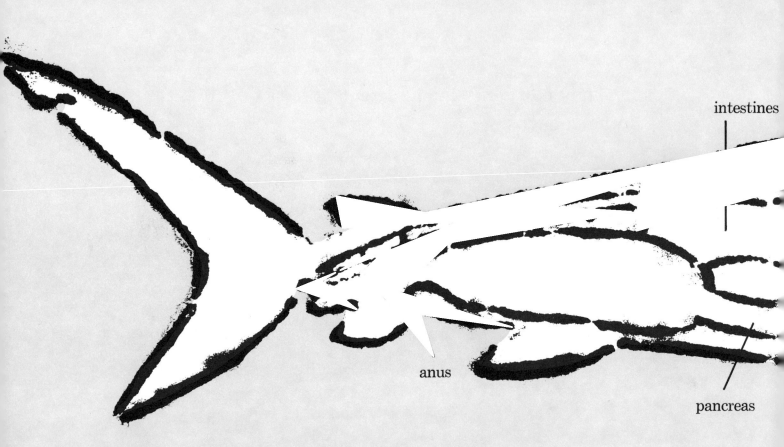

intestines

anus

pancreas

Sharks eat almost anything. Some sharks have bitten off people's arms and legs. Sometimes they eat things they cannot digest. Tar paper and tin cans have been found in their stomachs. One shark had a keg of nails in its stomach.

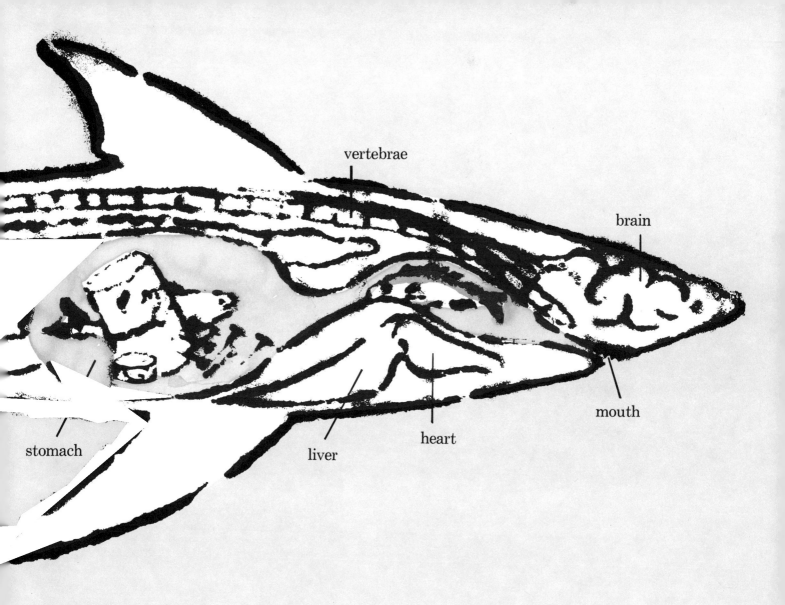

vertebrae

brain

mouth

heart

liver

stomach

5

6

Sometimes sharks use their eyes to find food.
Or they find food by sensing its movement in the
water. To do this they use their ears and their
"distance touch" sense. But mostly sharks find
their food by its smell. They can smell blood from
an injured fish. They can smell blood even when
the fish is far away.

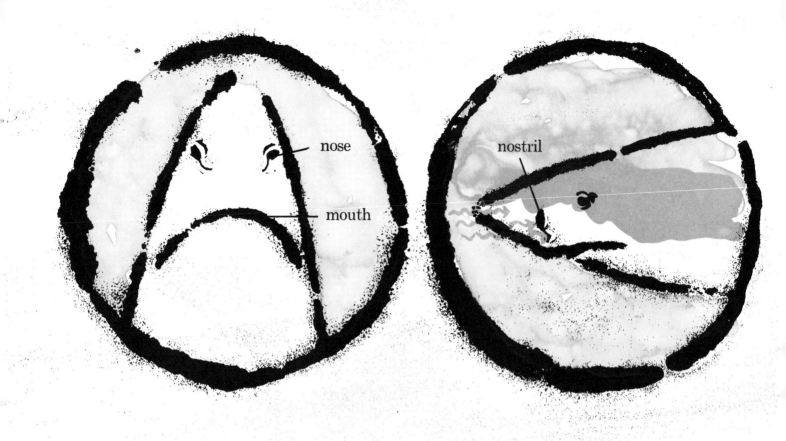

nose

mouth

nostril

A shark has a very good nose. The nose has two
outside openings. They are called nostrils. They
are in the shark's snout. There are extra folds of
skin in the openings. The folds help the shark
smell better. As the shark swims, water passes
through the nostrils.

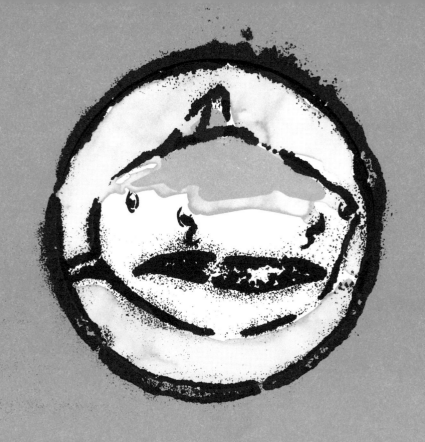

Scientists watch sharks to find out about them.
They watched a shark follow a wounded fish.
The fish swam in a straight line. It turned and
then swam straight again. A while later the shark
came along. The shark could not see the fish but it
swam along the exact path the fish had followed.
And it turned where the fish had turned. The
shark probably smelled blood that came from the
wounded fish.

Where there is no smell, sharks have other ways
to find food. They can feel the water movements
made by live food.

Sharks, and all other fish, have a "distance touch" sense called the lateral line system. The lateral line is made of hollow tubes or canals filled with a watery fluid. The canals are just under the skin. They contain sense cells like those in the ears. They run along the head and both sides of the shark's body, and they end at the tail. The canals have many tiny openings that look like stitches or dots on the surface of the skin.

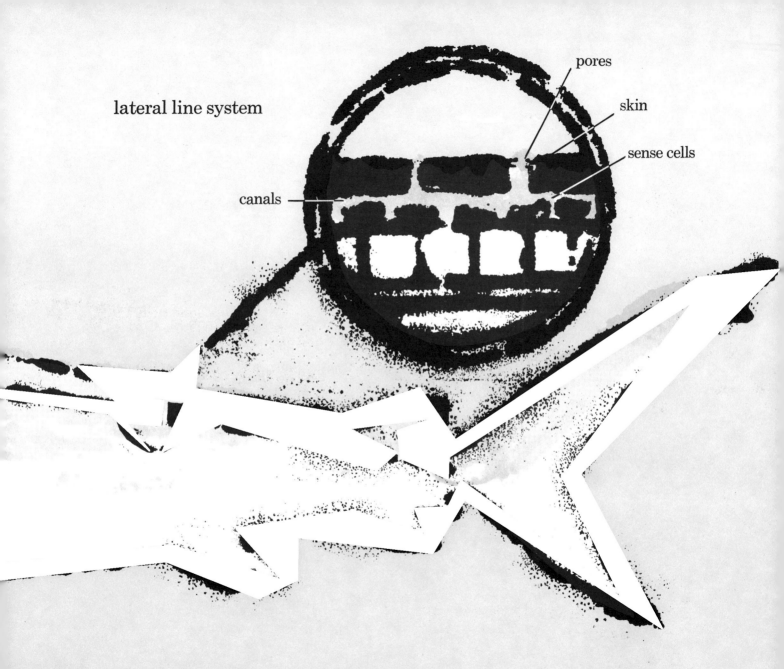

lateral line system

pores

skin

sense cells

canals

13

The sense cells in the canals of the lateral line system can "feel" movements in the water. Fish make sounds—clicks, rattles, and blurps. These sounds travel through the water as vibrations. The vibrations are sensed by the shark's ears and lateral line system. Then the shark knows there is food to be chased and caught. It follows the vibrations through the water. A shark can sense vibrations from as far away as 100 feet.

left ear of dogfish shark

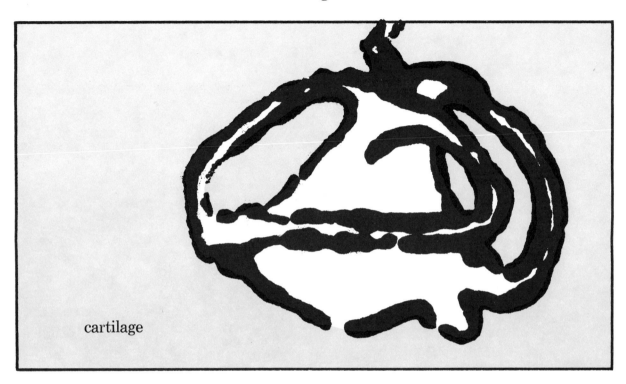

cartilage

All of a shark's ear is inside its head. A shark's ears don't look like yours or mine, but they work the same way. Next time you swim, put your head underwater. Have someone tap two stones together under the water. You will hear the sound clearly, but you may have trouble telling where

The shark's skeleton is cartilage, not bone.

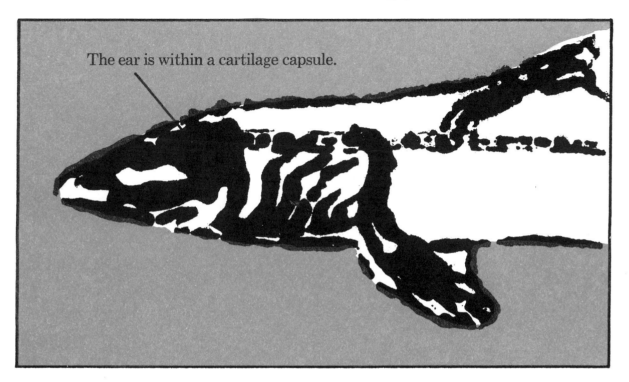

The ear is within a cartilage capsule.

it comes from. A shark would hear the sound and "feel" it too. So the shark would know its direction.

Scientists have tested the shark's hearing. When the underwater sounds are steady and regular, the shark gets used to them and pays little attention.

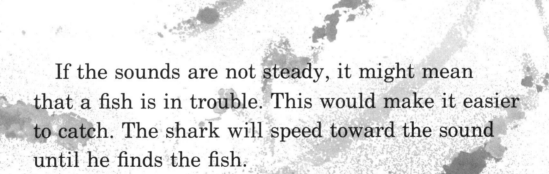

If the sounds are not steady, it might mean that a fish is in trouble. This would make it easier to catch. The shark will speed toward the sound until he finds the fish.

19

If the fish is hurt, the shark will circle it. Then it will strike, and eat the fish.

Scientists taped the sounds of a wounded fish. Later they played the tape underwater. The scientists flew overhead in a helicopter. They saw several sharks swimming around. As soon as the tape was started, each shark turned and swam toward the sound. When the tape was stopped the sharks stopped, too.

Sharks have other senses besides "distance touch." Scientists think sharks feel things with special cells in the skin of their snouts. They also have a special sense that detects very, very weak electrical currents.

Sometimes, because sharks swim fast, they may bump into things that are not alive. In a test, scientists put bricks where sharks could find them. The sharks bumped into the bricks. Maybe the sharks were hungry and were testing the bricks to see if they were good to eat.

25

26

Sometimes sharks do eat the wrong things. Perhaps this happens when the water they swim in is polluted. Maybe the shark that ate the tar paper and the tin cans gobbled them up along with his other food.

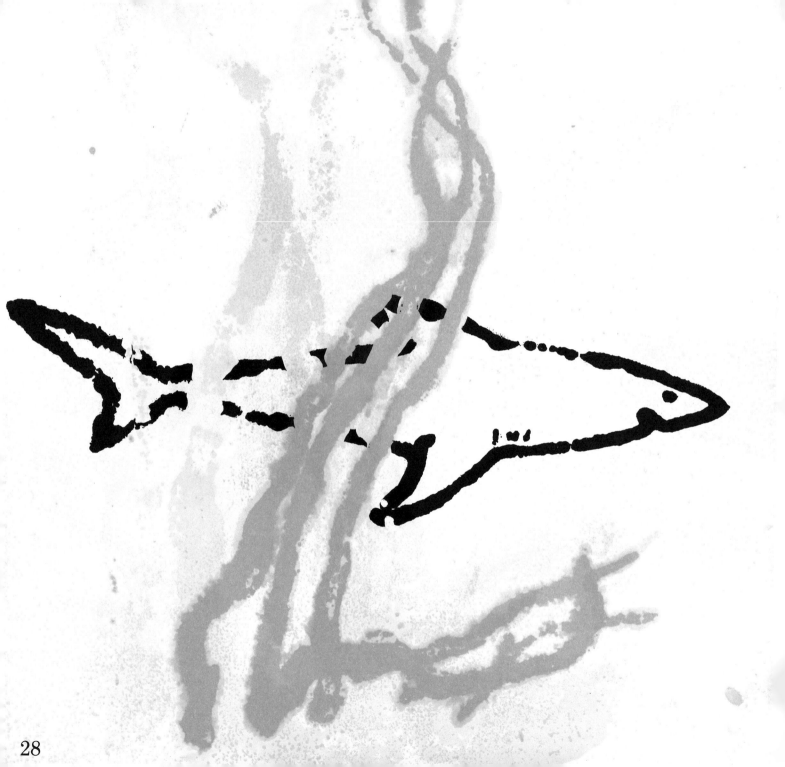

Sharks can smell food, they can feel and hear the water movements that food makes, and they can touch and taste food with special cells in their snouts, their mouths, and their skin. Sharks can see food, too.

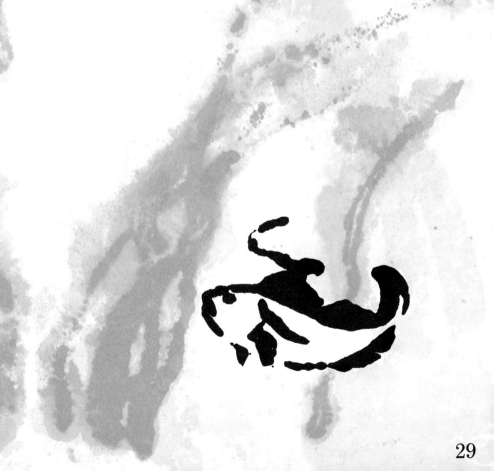

eye in the dark

Sharks' eyes are somewhat different from the eyes of other animals. They have both upper and lower eyelids. Most sharks can see in bright light and in dim light. Like a cat's eyes, the shark's eyes open wide and reflect light. Many sharks can see especially well in dim light. This is good because many of them feed mostly at night.

eye in the light

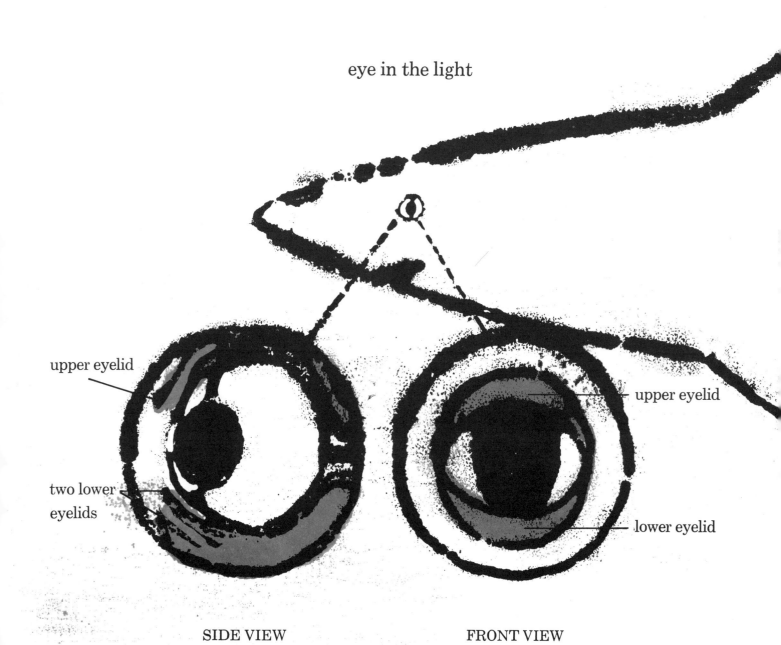

upper eyelid

two lower
eyelids

upper eyelid

lower eyelid

SIDE VIEW

FRONT VIEW

31

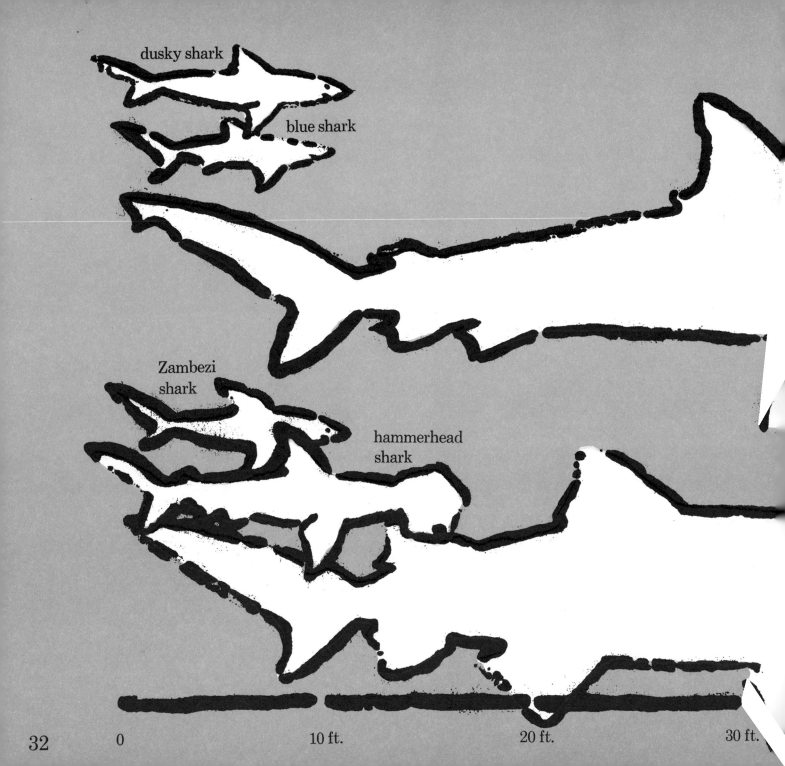

dusky shark

blue shark

Zambezi
shark

hammerhead
shark

0   10 ft.   20 ft.   30 ft.

basking shark

whale shark

Most sharks live in the ocean. Some live in rivers and lakes. There are about 250 different kinds of sharks in the world. All of them have good noses — so good that some scientists call sharks "swimming noses."

Sharks smell food, see food, touch food, and feel food, but mostly sharks eat food.

40 ft.   50 ft.

ABOUT THE AUTHOR

John F. Waters lives in a big old house on an island in Maine. From the window of his study he can watch windjammers and lobster boats as they set out to sea. The ocean has always been Mr. Waters' greatest interest, and nearly all of his books for young readers have dealt with marine subjects. His previous book in the Let's-Read-and-Find-Out series was *Green Turtle Mysteries,* and he has written on sea mammals, horseshoe crabs, eels, and giant sea creatures, among other subjects.

Mr. Waters was graduated from the University of Massachusetts and lived in Woods Hole on Cape Cod for twenty years. He has worked as a newspaperman and a teacher. With his wife and four children he now lives on Mt. Desert Island, Maine, and devotes all his time to writing.

ABOUT THE ILLUSTRATOR

When Ann Dalton was growing up, she spent all her summers at the seashore in Maine, and it was there that she first became interested in nature and the sea.

Ms. Dalton was born in Ossining, New York, and attended Pratt Institute in Brooklyn and Moore College of Art in Philadelphia. She has done illustrations for magazines and for *The New York Times,* has designed book jackets, and is the illustrator of a book on gardening.